SUPER CUTE!

Baby Kangaroos

by Megan Borgert-Spaniol

BELLWETHER MEDIA • MINNEAPOLIS, MN

Note to Librarians, Teachers, and Parents:

Blastoff! Readers are carefully developed by literacy experts and combine standards-based content with developmentally appropriate text.

Level 1 provides the most support through repetition of high-frequency words, light text, predictable sentence patterns, and strong visual support.

Level 2 offers early readers a bit more challenge through varied simple sentences, increased text load, and less repetition of high-frequency words.

Level 3 advances early-fluent readers toward fluency through increased text and concept load, less reliance on visuals, longer sentences, and more literary language.

Level 4 builds reading stamina by providing more text per page, increased use of punctuation, greater variation in sentence patterns, and increasingly challenging vocabulary.

Level 5 encourages children to move from "learning to read" to "reading to learn" by providing even more text, varied writing styles, and less familiar topics.

Whichever book is right for your reader, Blastoff! Readers are the perfect books to build confidence and encourage a love of reading that will last a lifetime!

This edition first published in 2017 by Bellwether Media, Inc.

No part of this publication may be reproduced in whole or in part without written permission of the publisher. For information regarding permission, write to Bellwether Media, Inc., Attention: Permissions Department, 5357 Penn Avenue South, Minneapolis, MN 55419.

Library of Congress Cataloging-in-Publication Data

Names: Borgert-Spaniol, Megan, 1989- author.
Title: Baby Kangaroos / by Megan Borgert-Spaniol.
Other titles: Blastoff! Readers. 1, Super Cute!
Description: Minneapolis, MN : Bellwether Media, Inc., [2017] | Series:
   Blastoff! Readers. Super Cute! | Audience: Ages 5-8. | Audience: K to
   grade 3. | Includes bibliographical references and index.
Identifiers: LCCN 2015043254 | ISBN 9781626173897 (hardcover : alk. paper)
Subjects: LCSH: Kangaroos–Infancy–Juvenile literature.
Classification: LCC QL737.M35 B67 2017 | DDC 599.2/22139–dc23
LC record available at http://lccn.loc.gov/2015043254

Printed in the United States of America, North Mankato, MN.

Table of Contents

Kangaroo Joey!

A baby kangaroo is called a joey. A **newborn** joey is the size of a grape.

The joey grows inside mom's **pouch**. After several months, it peeks out.

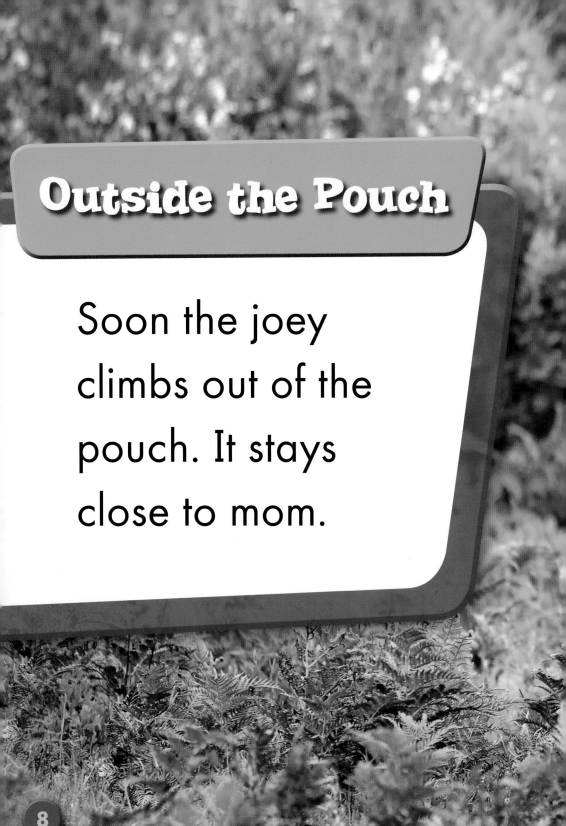

Outside the Pouch

Soon the joey climbs out of the pouch. It stays close to mom.

The joey learns how to hop. It has strong legs and large feet.

Care From Mom

Mom **grooms** her joey. She licks its fur clean.

She also gives her baby hugs. This is how they **bond**.

The joey rides in mom's pouch. It also **nurses** and sleeps there.

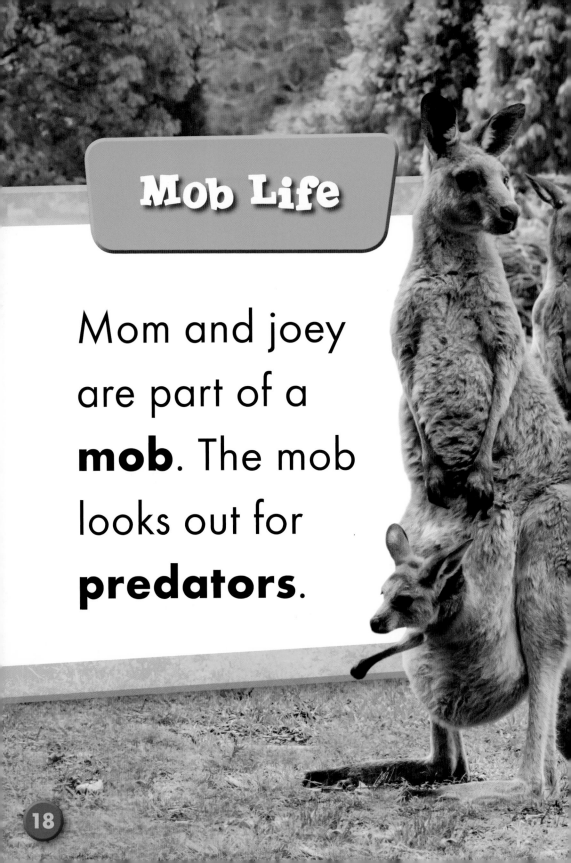

Mob Life

Mom and joey are part of a **mob**. The mob looks out for **predators**.

The joey jumps into mom's pouch when danger is near. You are safe now, joey!

Glossary

bond—to become close

grooms—cleans

mob—a group of kangaroos that travel together

newborn—just recently born

nurses—drinks mom's milk

pouch—a pocket of skin on the belly of a female kangaroo

predators—animals that hunt other animals for food

To Learn More

AT THE LIBRARY

Marsico, Katie. *A Kangaroo Joey Grows Up.*
New York, N.Y.: Children's Press, 2007.

Schuetz, Kari. *Kangaroos.* Minneapolis,
Minn.: Bellwether Media, 2013.

Stein, David Ezra. *Pouch!* New York, N.Y.:
G.P. Putnam's Sons, 2009.

ON THE WEB

Learning more about
kangaroos is as easy
as 1, 2, 3.

1. Go to www.factsurfer.com.

2. Enter "kangaroos" into the search box.

3. Click the "Surf" button and you will see a
list of related web sites.

With factsurfer.com, finding more information
is just a click away.

Index

The images in this book are reproduced through the courtesy of: K.A.Willis, front cover, pp. 6-7, 14-15 (top);
Danita Delimont/ Alamy, pp. 4-5; Jurgen & Christine Sohns/ FLPA, pp. 8-9; Radius Images/ Alamy,
pp. 10-11; Cyril Ruoso/ Minden Pictures/ Corbis, pp. 12-13; Tim Pryce Photography, pp. 14-15 (bottom);
Claudio Bertoloni, pp. 16-17; Westend61 GmbH/ Alamy, pp. 18-19; Kjuuurs, pp. 20-21.